AN UNOFFICIAL
JOKE BOOK
FOR
FORTNITERS

800 ALL-NEW EXPLOSIVELY HILARIOUS JOKES FOR FANS OF *FORTNITE*

AN UNOFFICIAL
JOKE BOOK
FOR
FORTNITERS

800 ALL-NEW EXPLOSIVELY HILARIOUS JOKES FOR FANS OF *FORTNITE*

BRIAN BOONE

ILLUSTRATED BY ALAN BROWN

Sky Pony Press
New York

Copyright © 2021 by Hollan Publishing, Inc.

All rights reserved. No part of this book may be reproduced in any manner without the express written consent of the publisher, except in the case of brief excerpts in critical reviews or articles. All inquiries should be addressed to Sky Pony Press, 307 West 36th Street, 11th Floor, New York, NY 10018.

Sky Pony Press books may be purchased in bulk at special discounts for sales promotion, corporate gifts, fund-raising, or educational purposes. Special editions can also be created to specifications. For details, contact the Special Sales Department, Sky Pony Press, 307 West 36th Street, 11th Floor, New York, NY 10018 or info@skyhorsepublishing.com.

Sky Pony® is a registered trademark of Skyhorse Publishing, Inc.®, a Delaware corporation.

Visit our website at www.skyponypress.com.

10 9 8 7 6 5 4 3 2 1

Library of Congress Control Number: 2021915999

Cover illustrations by Alan Brown
Cover design by Kai Texel

Paperback ISBN: 978-1-5107-6669-3
E-book ISBN: 978-1-5107-7083-6

Printed in the United States of America

CONTENTS

INTRODUCTION

Hey, boys and girls, ready to "drop" everything and chute and glide into the world of *Fortnite*? The game's popularity has spread around the world like a storm, the way that storm took over that colorful, fated island full of towers that tilt, springs full of salt, and lakes that are lazy. Except instead of turning people into zombies, it left the world wild about *Fortnite*, eager to compete against 99 friends and strangers to destroy monsters while dressed in a silly costume for the right to get to do a fun little dance at the end. Honestly, what's not to like?

Epic Games (and its millions of players) have made *Fortnite* a vast world full of interesting details. What's the "loot" from all this? Jokes! Here then is *An Unofficial Joke Book for Fortniters*, a second collection of quips, riddles, one-liners, puns, funny observations, and knock-knocks straight from The Island, personally delivered to you by the Battle Bus. Inside, you and your squad will find jokes about skins and characters, Cubes and Husks, mats and weapons, and every corner of *Fortnite* world and culture.

(You don't even need any V-bucks — and "noobs" are welcome, too!)

CHAPTER 1
POINTS OF INTEREST

Because in Fortnite, *the most important thing is location.*

Where do sore losers land on The Island?
Salty Springs.

•

How are parties like *Fortnite* lobbies?
Lots of stupid dance moves.

•

What do you get when you cross Slurpy Swamp with Misty Meadows?
Wet!

•

My friend says he found Burnout the first time he went to Steamy Stacks.
That sounds like a bunch of hot air to me.

I should've known Bunker Jonesy would be in Camp Cod.
Something smelled fishy.

•

What's the difference between a slob and *Fortnite*?
One wears dirty socks and the other has Dirty Docks.

•

WHAT'S FOR BREAKFAST AT
THE E.G.O. BARRACKS?

E.G.O. WAFFLES.

•

I'm headed to Razor Crest.
That's why I'm dressed so sharp!

Where can you find Reaper?
At Coral Reaps!

•

Why is *Fortnite* fun at Halloween?
Because of the Haunted Hills!

•

I was going to stalk around Lazy Lake.
But then I just didn't feel like it.

•

Where is it wet even if there isn't a storm?
Weeping Woods.

•

Where was the *Fortnite* player with no V-Bucks dropped into the game?
In the Peasant Park.

•

Where will you find beautiful birds in *Fortnite*?
Pheasant Park.

Why did Shrek start playing *Fortnite*?
Because he wanted to swing by the Slurpy Swamp.

•

Did you hear about the store fight in *Fortnite*?
It was a major Retail Row.

•

What's the hottest spot in *Fortnite*?
Sweaty Sands.

•

What do you say when you get to high ground?
"Hi, ground!"

•

The thing about elevators in *Fortnite*:
There are a lot of ups and downs.

•

What landmark in *Fortnite* are you destined to encounter?
Mount F8.

Have you been to Mowdown?
Not for a lawn time!

•

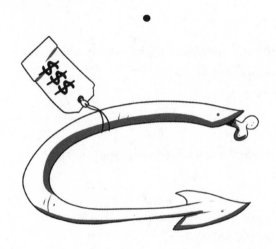

WHERE DID SHIVER GO
WHEN SHE LOST HER TAIL?

SHE WENT TO RE-TAIL ROW.

•

If you could land anywhere, where would you pick?
The Orchard!

Where's a good place to go for a rest?
Sheriff's Office!

•

What did the Fortniter say when she saw the Unremarkable Shack?
Nothing. Nothing at all.

•

What's a math teacher's favorite spot to land?
Zero Point.

•

Who loves the Shiver Inn?
Cole!

•

Where would you find new skins at the E.G.O. Hangar?
Hanging up!

•

Did you hear about the player who landed in Colossal Colosseum?
He really went for the gold!

Can you buy dust in *Fortnite*?
Sure, down at the Dusty Depo.

•

Where should you never seek medical help in *Fortnite*?
The Dirty Docks.

•

What's the most hostile place to land?
Quarrel Castle.

•

What happens if you replaced all the dirt in *Fortnite* with sugar?
You'd get Sweety Sands.

•

Where do they park the Battle Bus?
In the Pleasant Park-ing lot.

•

I was going to land in Steamy Stacks . . .
. . . but I just didn't have the energy.

●

They were going to put another tower of power in Steamy Stacks.
But they didn't want to over-react.

●

What do you drink when you land in Zero Point?
Crystal Light.

After dropping off warriors, the Battle Bus landed in Flush Factory.

It was stop #2.

•

Zero Point: it's like Kitty's version of Flush Factory.

Where in *Fortnite* would you find a cowboy?

At Corral Castle.

•

To what *Fortnite* location do you have to take a boat?

Retail Row.

•

What do you say to someone scavenging under Colossal Coliseum?

"Stair three well!"

•

What's the most dangerous plant in *Fortnite*?

The Power Plant.

What's full of trees but isn't Weeping Woods?
Stealthly Stronghold.

•

Why is it called Hotel 23?
So you don't get it confused with the other 22 hotels.

•

WHAT DID WINGTIP DO WHEN
SHE ARRIVED AT FLUSH FACTORY?

NOTHING — SHE WAS POOPED!

Where do you go to get into Bob's Bluff?
Bobby's Lobby.

•

What's longer than the word "queue"?
The *Fortnite* queue.

•

Where can you find the most ethical skins?
Down in Moral Reefs.

•

Where in *Fortnite* would you find trampolines?
Salty Springs!

•

Where does no one ever land?
Jilted Towers.

•

What area looks bad?
Tilted Glowers.

What's the oldest place on The Island?
Rusty Depot.

●

Where does the last player standing celebrate?
Lonely Lodge.

●

Who are the smartest people in Dirty Docks?
The Dirty Docktors.

●

Who are the best basketball players in *Fortnite*?
I don't know, but certainly not the Lazy Lakers!

●

What has eyes but cannot see?
The Island.

●

Where might you find football players in *Fortnite*?
Punter's Haven.

I like Butter Barn.
It's the cream of the crop!

●

Where might you mind a Valentine?
Flirty Docks.

●

WHAT'S THE GROSSEST THING
TO DRINK IN FORTNITE?

A SLURPY SWAMP SLURPEE.

Where can you find good building stones?
Dirty Rocks.

•

What's just opposite Weeping Woods?
Weeping Wouldn'ts.

•

What does Holly Hedges become at Christmas?
Jolly Hedges.

•

What does Lazy Lake become during The Storm?
Hazy Lake.

•

What plant can't you forage, no matter how hard you try?
The Power Plant!

•

Did you hear the one about the Unremarkable Shack?
It isn't worth repeating.

There used to be a bunch of Durr Burgers all over The Island.
Up until durr merger of Durr Burger.

●

Where does the music in *Fortnite* originate?
Choral Castle.

●

I heard Bob got to high ground.
But I think he's Bluffing!

●

What do you call someone who loots Durr Burger?
A hamburglar.

●

How could you celebrate a *Fortnite* win?
With a Block party!

Why'd they replace Risky Reels?

There was a new kid on The Block.

•

WHAT DO FORTNITERS CALL A BIG
BAG OF HOT FOOD?

STEAMY SNACKS!

What can you get to eat on The Block?
A square meal.

•

How can you get some exercise in *Fortnite*?
Run around The Block!

•

Did you hear about the new *Fortnite* movie?
It's a Block-buster.

•

FORTNITER #1: Are you crying?
FORTNITER #2: No, I'm just a little Misty!

•

What's the problem with the food in *Fortnite*?
It's too Salty!

•

What in *Fortnite* blows up but doesn't explode?
The Battle Bus's hot air balloon.

I know a *Fortnite*r who doesn't want to venture past the old Risky Reels site.
What a Block-head!

•

How does the day start in The Block?
With the rooster calling out "Block-a-doodle-doo!"

•

How is The Block like math?
Square roots!

•

Where can characters live in the town square?
Apartment Blocks.

•

What do you call a defender of The Island?
A Fort-Knight.

•

What's fortified and sounds like a trumpet?
Fort Crumpet.

CHAPTER 2
THE SKINNY ON SKINS

All about the characters that make Fortnite *so much fun.*

Did you hear about the guy who made a fortune inventing *Fortnite*?
Talk about a Mogul Master.

•

If you find yourself falling behind the competition, try playing as Tomatohead.
He'll help you ketchup!

•

Do you like the way Beef Boss looks?
Yes, a tongue!

•

How do you locate Synth Star?
Just tap your keyboard!

When is a success in *Fortnite* a bad situation?

When you reached Tier 100, and it gets Dire.

●

WHAT CHARACTER CAN YOU
JUST BUILD YOURSELF?

KIT!

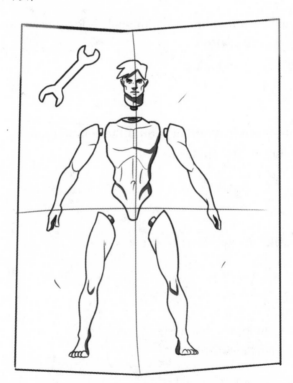

How do you make Reese's Pieces in *Fortnite*?
Let Reese throw a bomb into a building.

•

FORTNITER #1: Guess what character I want to play as.
FORTNITER #2: Bullseye?
**FORTNITER #1: Yeah, that's what I'll say if you guess
    right.**

•

What skin should you wear to get wood and stone?
A har-vest!

•

I was going to play as the winter-themed character . . .
. . . but then I didn't have any V-Bucks, so Snowman-do.

•

**What do you get when you cross a mermaid with a
    soldier?**
An Arial Assault Trooper.

FORTNITER #1: Did you get The Mighty Volt skin?
FORTNITER #2: I didn't have V-Bucks, so I charged it.

•

What kind of locks are on the buildings in *Fortnite*?
Hemlocks.

•

Where does Bunker Jonesy go for a rest?
To his Bunker beds.

•

What would you get if you combined Fishstick and Bigfoot?
I don't know, but it probably wouldn't smell very good.

•

What would you get if you combined Farmer Steel and Tomatohead?
A big harvest.

What do you call it when a squad of Ravens knocks out a player?

A murder of crows.

●

Why do hippies like the *Fortnite* character Reese?

Because they just want to give Reese a chance.

●

What happened when Reese fell asleep in her battle armor?

It got covered with Reese's creases.

●

FORTNITER #1: Do you like Peely?

FORTNITER #2: Yes, a bunch!

●

I missed out on my chance to play as Fishstick.

But it's okay, there are plenty of other fish in the sea.

I thought about playing as the banana character.
But I just couldn't see the a-Peel.

•

I'M PLAYING AS TRIGGERFISH.
I'M REALLY GUNNING FOR VICTORY!

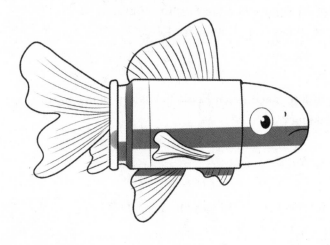

•

Tomatohead was running behind the rest of the crew until splat, he got hit.
The other player said, "Ketchup."

What does Kit eat?
Kit-Kats.

●

I recently played a game as Doggo.
He's a very good player. He's a good boy! *Yes he is! Yes he is!*

●

I thought about playing as Farmer Steel.
I don't know, though. He seems hard.

●

A shot hit the detective character right in the mouth.
Right in Sleuth's tooth, and that's the truth!

●

What happens if you eat an onion while listening to hip-hop?
You get Rapscallion.

●

I was going to play as the ventriloquist doll character.
But then I realized that I'm no Dummy.

FORTNITER #1: Have you ever played as Blaze?
FORTNITER #2: No way, it's too hot.

•

What do you call a boy who wins *Fortnite* a lot?
Victor.

•

Cole went into Durr Burger.
"Sorry, we don't serve you here," said the manager.
"Why not?"
"We have a rule about it, it's right on the menu."
"Yeah, what's it called?"
"Coleslaw."

•

BRUTUS: Hey, there's something weird on your head!
BEEF BOSS: It's okay. Olive.

•

I thought you'd be excited that I got the Snowmando skin.
But you seem a little frosty.

Where can you find Doggo?
In a doghouse, probably!

•

What song does Snowmando sing?
"Walkin' like a winter wonder-man!"

•

What's the difference between Peely and Brutus?
One is fruit and the other's a brute!

•

How does Lexa get to The Island?
In her Lexus.

•

What do you call a little Mandalorian?
Boydalorian.

•

My *Fortnite* skin witnessed the Volcano Event.
He felt so guilty, he couldn't lava with himself.

What kind of music does Farmer Steel listen to?
Metal!

●

You have to use your V-Bucks to get the farmer skin.
You can't Steel it.

●

I JUST ENCOUNTERED A GIANT
TEDDY BEAR IN FORTNITE.

IT LEFT ME IN STITCHES.

What happens if you cross Deadfire and Blaze?
Burnout!

•

Why did they call him Big Chuggus?
Because if he was little, that would have been a silly name.

•

Why are skeletons bad at *Fortnite*?
No skins.

•

How does a Fortniter eat fried chicken?
They only take the skins.

•

How do you grab Fishstick?
Try baiting him!

•

What does Peely say when he's sick?
"I'm not peeling well."

How do you catch fish in *Fortnite*?
With a Fishstick.

•

How does Ninja know where to find enemies in *Fortnite*?
Because he wears Sneakers.

•

Why can't you see Ninja?
Because he's really good at being a ninja.

•

Want to hear a joke about Beef Boss?
Maybe you don't, it's pretty cheesy.

•

What do you call it when one Beef Boss meets another?
A meating!

•

I was going to play with Beef Boss.
But him and me, we've got beef.

Where does Tomatohead hang out?
The salad bar.

•

What skin doesn't think eating vegetables is healthy?
Tomatohead!

•

Who is covered in ash but has not burned?
Tomatohead — he has a "must-ash."

•

FORTNITER #1: Is Bunker Jonesy a good skin?
FORTNITER #2: Sure, he's a slam bunk!

•

FORTNITER #1: Is Bunker Jonesy a good skin?
FORTNITER #2: Nah, it's a bunch of bunk.

•

What kind of wood does Fishstick find?
Fishsticks!

Who has big "feats" even if they lose?
Bigfoot!

•

WHO SOUNDS LIKE A WEAPON
BUT IS REALLY A CHARACTER?

SHOGUN.

•

Snowmando played great today.
He put on quite the snow.

•

What skin is smart but stupid?
Dummy!

Why'd they put Sleuth in the game?
It's a mystery!

•

Who's the most inquisitive skin?
Tomatohead, because he mustache you a question.

•

I don't want to play as the spider-woman skin.
I have Arachne-phobia!

•

FORTNITER #1: Have you played as Crackshot?
FORTNITER #2: No, that's nuts!

•

What do you call two Cyclos?
A bi-cyclo!

•

FORTNITER #1: Did you play as that one hooded skin?
FORTNITER #2: I did. I guess it was Fate!

Who has the most books in *Fortnite*?
The Read Knight.

•

When is The Storm not a storm?
When it's Tempest.

•

When would you find spiders in the daytime in *Fortnite*?
When it's Spider Knight.

•

What do you call a foraging Peely?
Fruit that loots.

•

I can't believe I never found Peely.
It's bananas!

•

What character always falls for baiting?
Fishstick!

I RECENTLY ACQUIRED THE
SASQUATCH CHARACTER.

WHAT A FEET!

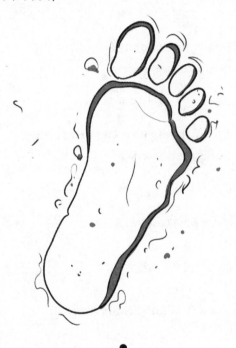

When are the 80s the 90s?

When you're playing as Aerobic Assassin.

Did you hear about the *Fortnite* pony party?
It was quite the Bash.

•

When is a bunny not a bunny?
When it's Chief Hopper.

•

FORTNITER #1: I got you a Candyman skin.
FORTNITER #2: How sweet!

•

Who makes the best coffee?
Grind!

•

What skin doesn't mind sticking around?
Gumshoe!

•

Who's the dumbest?
Hollowhead!

What happens if you put Burger Boss in a moving cube?
It makes an Olive-vator.

•

Did you hear about Blaze?
She got elected to the *Fortnite* Hall of Flame.

•

What do you get when you cross Blaze with a black hole?
Fire in the hole!

•

What did Blaze say when she landed on The Island?
"This is fire!"

•

What does Spider Knight drink for energy?
Apple Spider.

•

What's Red and smells like apples?
Red Knight holding an apple.

What kind of skin can find corn?
A Colonel!

●

Can you put a skin on Flush Factory?
Sure, if it's a costume potty.

●

What character loves Thanksgiving?
Turk!

●

I used to play as Centurion.
But not for like 100 years.

●

Who can climb structures the best?
Scaley!

●

I can't believe Cobalt lost.
He really blue it.

Chomp Sr. spread rumors about me.
What a big mouth!

•

Chomp Sr. spread rumors about me.
But he says it's all tooth.

•

I picked the warrior princess skin.
It felt like a good Hime.

•

What's the difference between a condor and Kondor?
A condor is endangered and Kondor will endanger you!

•

What's a father's favorite *Fortnite* skin?
Dadfire.

•

Whenever you play as Bigfoot, you have put the game on paws.

How can you tell if Bigfoot is near?
Big footprints.

●

What kind of skin would Bigfoot use?
Skin? He's got too much hair to ever see any skin.

●

What mod can you get for Bigfoot?
Big shoes!

●

FORTNITER #1: Have you seen Bigfoot?
FORTNITER #2: Not yeti!

●

What food does Bigfoot plant?
Sas-squash.

●

How does Bigfoot tell time?
With a sasqu-watch.

WHAT GAME IS RAZOR GOOD AT?

FORTNITE: SHAVE THE WORLD.

How is real Bigfoot like *Fortnite* Bigfoot?

He's hard to find!

FORTNITER #1: Do you think I can win with this skin?

FORTNITER #2: It's a Longshot.

What would you get if Reese went to "The Pit"?
Reese's Pizzas!

•

Jack Gourdon was my brother, and he excelled with weapons.
He was One-Pump-Kin.

•

I was going to play as that one Steamy Stacks character.
But then I felt Burnout.

•

You went with Sparkplug?
Shocking!

•

I was going to use Kondor.
But then I didn't think it was going to fly.

•

FORTNITER #1: Where's Farmer Steel?
FORTNITER #2: You Steem to think I'm going to tell you.

Is it easy to grab a new character in *Fortnite*?
Sure, you're skin and out.

•

What beauty product do Fortniters use?
Skin cream.

•

What skin would you find up a tree?
Bamboo-sled.

•

Who do you call when your skins aren't working?
A dermatologist.

CHAPTER 3
WELCOME, MATS!

Feel free to "loot" this collection of jokes about Fortnite *equipment.*

Did I tell you I got a new glider skin the other day?
It was a real Picnic!

•

What do you call searching for snipers in *Fortnite*?
Hunting Rifles.

•

What is a *Fortnite* gamer's favorite Disney character?
Scar.

•

FORTNITER #1: How do I destroy a tree?
FORTNITER #2: Hey, just axe.
FORTNITER #1: I did!

WELCOME, MATS!

Are there a lot of harvesting tools in *Fortnite*?
Sure, take your pick!

•

I'm going out to get supplies.
I'm planning on a chopping spree!

•

That wood was hard to get.
I really had to go out on a limb.

•

Does *Fortnite* have commercials?
No, but it's full of ADS.

•

When do you log on when you're still playing *Fortnite*?
When you obtain wood.

•

What can you keep in a Rusty Can?
Whatever you want, as long as it's rusty.

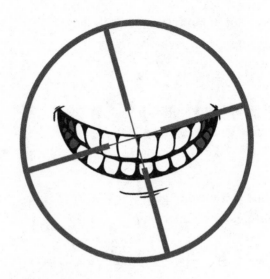

WHY DO FORTNITE PLAYERS HAVE
GREAT SMELLING BREATH?

THEY USE SCOPE.

•

What's a great Halloween game in *Fortnite*?
Bombing for apples.

•

**What do you get when you cross a Sledgehammer with
   some apples?**
Applesauce!

Reel talk:
Where in *Fortnite* do I find a fishing rod?

•

Mushrooms were a great addition to *Fortnite*.
What a fungi!

•

What food would you find in the Battle Bus?
Mushroom!

•

What did the Fortniter name her fishing pole?
Rod.

•

What did the Fortniter do after she got a fishing rod and another Harvesting Tool?
She reel-axed.

•

What's as sharp as an arrow?
Another arrow.

That player got knocked even though he had a great weapon.
I guess it's Armature hour.

•

I love using the Harpoon Gun.
What can I say? I'm hooked!

•

What room can't you build in *Fortnite*?
A mushroom.

•

What do V-Bucks and butterflies have in common?
They both seem to just fly away!

•

Did you know that Harry Potter is a Fortniter?
He's got a Scar, right?

•

What do you call a Harvesting Tool that loves you?
An axe-girlfriend!

FORTNITER #1: Are these all the harvesting tools?
FORTNITER #2: Sure, take your pick!

●

WHY DID THE FORTNITE PLAYER
BUILD A HOUSE OUT OF OLD
HARVESTED WOOD?

HE NEEDED STRUCTURE.

How do Fortniters cover up their body odor?
Axe body spray.

•

When is a good tool also terrible?
When it's the Abominable Axe.

•

What do Fortniters do with their leftovers?
They wrap them in Airfoil.

•

What gum do Fortniters chew?
Trident.

•

How do Fortniters take their pizza?
With Axeroni.

•

Why did the Fortniter go to Mexico?
He wanted to see the Axetec ruins.

How does a Fortniter cut fish?
With a Bait Bones.

•

What terrifies Peely?
Bananaxe!

•

FORTNITER #1: What should I do with this skull-shaped axe?
FORTNITER #2: I don't know, use your Noggin!

•

What kind of axe might you find near the Flush Factory?
Bottom Feeder!

•

What's a Fortniter's favorite football team?
The Chargers.

•

Does a Fortniter ever calm down?
No, but they'll Chill-Axe.

WHAT'S IT CALLED WHEN
THE BUN-HEAD FIRES AN ARROW?

A CROSS-BAO.

Where can you find crows in *Fortnite*?
At the Crowbar.

Ever used the drum-shaped axe?
It can't be beat! (Actually, it can.)

How many Driver axes can you buy?
Fore!

●

FORTNITER #1: Why did you buy the Elite Cleat axe?
FORTNITER #2: For kicks!

●

What kind of pizza do Fortniters order?
A Pair-peronni.

●

I like the Piranhas tool.
It's got bite!

●

Are the V-Bucks weapons good?
They're a Slam Dunk!

●

FORTNITER #1: I got a Vision tool!
FORTNITER #2: Yeah, I can see that.

How can you buy a Vox without V-Bucks?
You just buy an Ox.

●

They were going to release a new, superior assault rifle.
But then they suppressed it.

●

I bought a Heavy Assault Rifle.
But now it's really weighing on me.

●

What makes it a Scoped Assault Rifle?
It smells like mint!

●

What sounds like a weapon for *Fortnite* noobs?
Infantry Rifle.

●

What kind of sandwich does a Jellyfish make?
A peanut butterfish and Jellyfish sandwich.

FORTNITER #1: I thought you were getting a Skye's Assault Rifle?
FORTNITER #2: It's up in the air.

●

I ran into a Thermal Fish.
And then everything went white!

●

WHAT WEAPON WORKS
UNDERWATER?

A SUBMACHINE GUN.

I lost my chance to buy a Revolver.
But these things tend to come back around.

•

Why did Cuddle Team Leader go after Skull Trooper with a pickaxe?
It had a bone to pick.

•

What's the first thing you should do if you're going to chop wood in *Fortnite*?
Pickaxe.

•

What instrument does Funk Ops play in the *Fortnite* band?
The Axe-o-phone.

•

Why did Jonesy cut down the tree if he didn't need wood?
He didn't mean to — it was an axe-ident.

Did you hear about the new *Fortnite* character with a Harvesting Tool stuck in his head?

His name is Axel.

●

What happened to Axel when he got his pickaxe stuck in his head?

A splitting headache.

●

Why are kid Fortniters so good at finding mats?

Because they're "minors."

●

What do you have to pick before it can pick?

A Pickaxe.

●

You might describe me as being extremely sharp, yet I don't actually have a brain. What am I?

A Pickaxe.

FORTNITER #1: I bought a Vuvuzela.
FORTNITER #2: That sounds terrible!

•

What rises before it falls?
A Pickaxe.

•

You're stuck inside your structure. All you have is a pickaxe. How do you get out?
Unlock the house and walk out!

•

Why was the *Fortnite* player mad at the tree?
He had an Axe to grind.

•

What rock band do Fortniters enjoy the most?
AC/DC.

•

FORTNITER #1: Is High Seas easy to find?
FORTNITER #2: No, it's harrrrrrrrd.

Of course I can't stop playing *Fortnite*.
It's got Heavy Hooks!

•

What goes inside the Flush Factory?
A really big Plunja.

•

Where can you find gold bars?
In rich soil.

•

What do you get when you cross Fishstick with a bar?
Goldfish!

•

What happened when Bunny Brawler found a ton of gold?
She became a million-hare.

•

FORTNITER #1: Did you do 10 damage with that weapon?
FORTNITER #2: Yeah, I'm pumped!

WHAT HAPPENS IF YOU THROW
A BAR AT A CARROT STICK?

YOU GET 14-CARROT GOLD!

How did X feel after finding a bunch of gold bars?
Gilty.

What kind of gold does Doggo like?
Barks.

What kind of gold does Spider Knight prefer?
Barbs.

•

What kind of gold does Farmer Steel find?
Gold barns.

•

Is the Pirate Cannon a temporary thing?
No, it's canon!

•

FORTNITER #1: Are you picking your nose?
FORTNITER #2: No, I'm "harvesting."

•

What do you call two Fortniters?
Pair-a-shooters!

•

What kind of stone do knocked players get?
Tomb-stone.

FORTNITER #1: Why did you use a small shield potion instead of a shield potion?
FORTNITER #2: I wasn't that thirsty.

●

I love *Fortnite* potions.
They always stir me up.

●

I'm not saying potions cause accidents
But they always make you wet yourself.

●

Who could make potions?
Brew-tis.

●

What do you call the songs on the radio in carts?
Cart-Tunes!

●

What can you eat during a cart ride?
Fast food.

What do you get if you cross *Fortnite* fish with a cart?
A crustacean wagon.

•

I was almost shot by that guy with the crossbow . . .
Fortunately, I arrowly escaped.

•

Did you hear about the cart that didn't work?
It was a Brokeswagon.

•

I thought I wanted a *Fortnite* vehicle.
But at the end of the day, I didn't have the cart.

•

I wrote a book about the *Fortnite* carts.
It's an auto-biography.

•

***Fortnite* makers weren't sure about including piñatas.**
But they really blew up!

WHAT DO YOU CALL A
LLAMA'S MOTHER?

A LLAMAMAMA.

MOM

What do you call a piñata without anything in it?
A llama.

Why don't you have to feed the Llamas in *Fortnite*?
Because they're already full.

WELCOME, MATS!

FORTNITER #1: Do you think piñatas are the best thing in *Fortnite*?
FORTNITER #2: Nah, they can be beat.

•

The Llama got so mad after it was robbed of its candy.
It yelled out, "I've been fleeced!"

•

Did you hear about the piñata upset her candy was taken?
What a Llama queen!

What do Llamas call The Storm?
Llamageddon!

•

What cereal do *Fortnite*rs eat for breakfast?
Froot Loots.

•

Did you hear they're leaving axes out of the new season?
They got cut.

**I really liked that hamster wheel vehicle they had in
Fortnite.**
I had a Baller!

•

**What do you get when you cross a small metal cart with a
helicopter?**
A Chopping Cart.

•

What's the most boring vehicle in *Fortnite*?
A Drift-bored.

•

**I was so excited when I found that Holiday Harvesting
tool that I swung it around.**
I raised my hams in the air like I just don't care!

•

What do toddlers and Fortniters have in common?
They spend a lot of time playing with Blocks.

I've gotten much better at the Build.
You could say I've ramped it up.

•

I'm surprised by how easily I learned the Build.
I was floored!

•

How can you spot a Fortniter at Starbucks?
They order everything with one pump.

•

How do Fortniters get an energy boost?
With a Rocket Lunch.

•

What's wrong with the food in *Fortnite*?
Too much assault!

•

What sport do Fortniters like?
Boxing!

I love *Fortnite* so much.
I wish I could box it up!

●

How is this book like *Fortnite*?
Sooner or later, you're going to come across a Bad Joke.

CHAPTER 4
MONSTER-OUS JOKES

Be aware: This part of the book is loaded with Husks!

How can you tell the difference between a regular person and a Husk?

A husk's shorts are blue!

•

Why are Beehive Husks so assertive?

Because they were always told to just bee themselves.

•

What monsters are the most wanted in *Fortnite*?

Beehive Husks. There was a lot of buzz about them.

•

What grades did Hive Husks get in school?

Mostly Bees.

Why are Husks so relentless?
They're just very dead-icated.

●

Did you hear about the Husk cow?
It was moo-tated!

●

Where are you on The Island if you encounter a group of Husks?
A dead end.

●

What room should you build to avoid Husks?
A living room.

●

What does a character have in common with attacking Husks?
They're both dead meat!

WHAT WEAPONS DO HUSKS LIKE?

CROSSBONES.

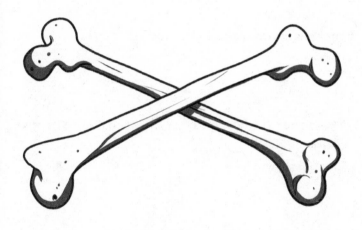

What time do Husks prefer to attack?
Ate o'clock.

Where do *Fortnite* zombies buy their clothes?
At the Husky store.

Why do monsters stalk The Island?
Husk because!

•

What kind of zombies are Hive Husks?
Zom-bees.

•

What do you get when you cross Bunker Jonesy with a Husk?
A guy with a beard hive.

What's black and white and dead all over?
A Husk in a tuxedo.

•

What do you get if you cross Tomatohead with a Husk?
Marinara!

FORTNITER #1: I wish you could smell what's happening in *Fortnite*.

FORTNITER #2: Why? So you could get a whiff of the food at Durr Burger?

FORTNITER #1: No, so you could sense zombies before they attacked.

FORTNITER #2: Ah, the musk of a husk!

•

What do you call a Husk with lots of little Husklings around?

A mom-ster.

•

ON WHAT DAY WILL HUSKS ATTACK?

CHEWSDAY.

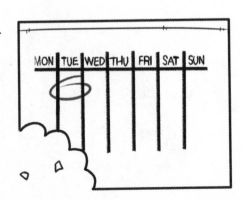

How easy is it to take down Husks in *Fortnite*?
It's a no-brainer.

•

What would you get if you crossed a Husk with Snowmando?
Frostbite.

•

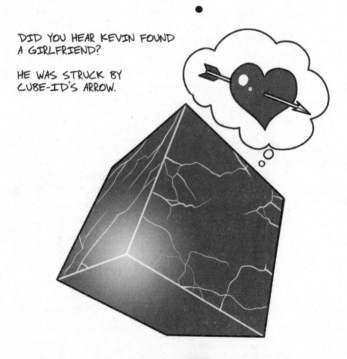

DID YOU HEAR KEVIN FOUND A GIRLFRIEND?

HE WAS STRUCK BY CUBE-ID'S ARROW.

Why don't Husks like jokes?
Their sense of humor is rotten.

•

What do you call a Husk with a bell around its neck?
A dead ringer.

•

When do Husks in *Fortnite* sleep?
Only if they're dead tired.

•

What happened when a Husk attacked a cow?
It turned into zom-beef.

•

What do you do if a mob of 100 Husks surrounds your structure?
Hope that all 100 Battle Royale players are nearby.

•

Where do Husks buy their torn pants?
At the torn pants store.

Why is corn so hard to get in *Fortnite*?
Because it's hiding behind the Husks.

•

What's white, smooth, and deadly?
A Flush Factory invested with Husks.

•

Why are Husks after your player anyway?
They want your skin!

•

What do you call it when a monster approaches as The Storm grows nearer?
A Husk at dusk!

•

That monster finished me off quickly.
It was a brusque Husk.

•

What candy do Beehive Husks eat?
Jelly Bees.

What other game would you find Hive Husks?
A spelling bee!

•

WHAT DO YOU CALL A
HUSKLING IN A SHRUB?

A BUSH BABY!

•

Do Husks ever rest?
Of corpse they don't!

Why do Husks hunt players?
It's a matter of corpse.

•

In a poll to name the most liked characters in *Fortnite*, Husks came in . . .
. . . dead last.

•

One day the Husks didn't show up to The Island.
They were just feeling too rotten.

•

Why do Husks prefer living characters?
They only like flesh ingredients.

•

Did you hear the husks opened a Subway in *Fortnite*?
Eat flesh!

FORTNITER #1: Do you like Sploder Husks?

FORTNITER #2: Sure, they're the bomb!

Fortnite **wasn't too popular until they added variations of monsters.**

Yep, those Sploder Husks really blew up!

•

What would you call it if a giant monster used the Flush Factory?

An incoming toxic storm!

•

What game can you play with *Fortnite* **monsters?**

Hive and Seek.

•

What you call the leader of the Hive Husks?

The Queen Bee.

Why is The Cube named Kevin?
Because that's its name, silly.

•

Was The Cube a major event?
Sure, it started a Kevolution!

•

What does The Cube consume?
Energy drinks.

•

What else does The Cube consume?
Square meals.

•

What position would Kevin play in football?
Cube-Bee.

•

Is The Cube tough?
Well, he can certainly box.

HOW CAN YOU TELL THAT A
SPLODER WANTS TO HURT YOU?

THEIR PRO-PANE.

Don't be afraid of The Cube.

After all, there are six sides to every story.

What does Kevin do when he wants to chill?
He goes from Cube to Ice Cube.

•

How does The Cube use butterflies to teleport characters?
He uses C-Uber.

•

What type of dancing does Kevin like?
Square dancing.

•

Where does Kevin go when he's feeling worn out?
Jiffy Cube.

•

Where was Kevin born?
Cube-a.

•

Why is Kevin the edgiest figure in *Fortnite*?
Because he literally has the most edges — 12 in all.

Why is The Cube so devastating?
Because every place he touches, he runes.

•

How do you know The Cube can play the guitar?
Because when he saw one, he Rift!

•

Why should you never hang out near The Cube?
Because your mother always said to avoid the Rift-wrath.

•

How big was Kevin, exactly?
I don't know, but I bet it's a lot of cubits.

•

What do you call Kevin in the snow?
An Ice Cube.

•

How do you destroy Kevin?
With a Butterfly Knife!

WHAT WOULD YOU GET IF YOU
CROSSED A HUSK WITH SNOWMANDO?

FROSTBITE.

What's Kevin's favorite *Fortnite* gaming type?
Butterfly Royale!

•

Why was the Husk denied entry at Durr Burger?
It wasn't wearing a shirt.

•

What do Husks and these jokes have in common?
They're brainless.

CHAPTER 5
A VERY EMOTE-TIONAL CHAPTER

Good news: you don't have to win a game of Fortnite *or wait until the end to try out these jokes about emotes!*

How can you emote remotely?

When you "Phone It In."

•

I've been wanting more emotes lately.

So I decided to "Step It Up."

•

When is a salty player not salty?

When they get the "Pure Salt" emote.

•

Do you like the "Backstroke"?

Yes, it's going swimmingly.

When is a winning game broken?
When you're "Breakin'"!

•

You don't have to emote forever.
A little "Dab" is plenty.

•

FORTNITER #1: What's your favorite emote?
FORTNITER #2: "It's Complicated."
FORTNITER #1: Come on, just tell me.

•

I just got that flag-based emote.
After all, it was a "Banner" victory!

•

I like the "Blinding Lights" emote.
But I only do it on The Weeknd.

•

I didn't want to spend my V-Bucks on emotes.
But then I reached my "Breaking Point."

FORTNITER #1: I can't decide which emote to get.
FORTNITER #2: Go on, "Brush Your Shoulders Off."
FORTNITER #1: I will, but I don't know which emote to get!

•

What's the most redundant emote?
"Bulletproof," because you've just proven that you are with the victory!

•

I was going to get an emote.
And then I got "Busy."

•

I had just enough V-Bucks to get the emote I want.
It was all so very "Calculated."

•

Hey, when you're ready to decide on an emote . . .
"Call Me."

FORTNITER #1: Which emote should I get?

FORTNITER #2: "Coin Flip"?

FORTNITER #1: Then I'd have to decide between two!

●

I THOUGHT I WANTED THE "BALLSY" EMOTE.

BUT AS IT TURNS OUT, I COULDN'T JUGGLE IT.

●

PARENT: What's an emote?

FORTNITER: I'm "Confused."

PARENT: Me too!

When is a good thing dark?
When it's a winning "Dark Side" emote.

●

What do happy *Fortnite* players do with their chips?
They "Dip"!

●

I had a hard time picking an emote.
I guess I was "Distracted."

●

FORTNITER #1: Did you like my emote?
FORTNITER #2: Stop "Fishin'"!

●

Did you like my emote?
I think it's "Flippin' Incredible!"

●

What's the "Focused" emote doing on his phone, anyway?
Playing *Fortnite*.

"Freewheelin'" got placed into *Fortnite* at the last minute.
It just skated on in!

●

When does Fortnite begin *and* end with a storm?
When you select the "Gale Force" emote!

●

FORTNITER #1: Do you want to pick an emote or what?
FORTNITER #2: "Hang On."
FORTNITER #1: No, decide now!

●

Do you know the "Hoppity" emote?
It gets me very eggs-cited!

●

"I Declare!" is a great emote.
Big fan!

What's the sludgiest of all emotes?
An e-moat.

•

FORTNITER #1: What's your favorite emote?
FORTNITER #2: It's "Go Time!"
**FORTNITER #1: Come on, you can pick *something*
    before we play again.**

•

I grabbed a new emote.
After all, it was a "Job Well Done."

•

What's Peely's favorite emote?
"Nana Nana."

•

Which emote is your favorite?
Or should I "Point It Out"?

What do victorious *Fortnite* players eat?

"Pop Locks."

•

Did you hear that they were going to make a *Fortnite* TV show?

It got canceled when someone did a "Showstopper."

•

WHAT SHOULD YOU DO WHEN YOU "WADDLE AWAY"?

DUCK!

Did you hear there are evil wizards in *Fortnite*?
They're "Slitherin'!"

•

I thought I'd won the game.
But then there was a "Twist."

•

I like the "Unicycle" emote.
It's a wheely big deal.

•

What do you call "We Are Venom"?
A symbiote emote!

•

I had a great *Fortnite* session today.
From beginning to victory to emote, it was a "Whirlwind"!

•

FORTNITER #1: Where'd you get that emote?
FORTNITER #2: It must be "Witchcraft."

I wanted to get a "Pumpernickel."
But I didn't have enough bread.

•

A friend and I played *Fortnite* online.
We celebrated e-motely.

•

FORTNITER #1: Happy with your new emote?
FORTNITER #2: It's Dynamite.
FORTNITER #1: Which one did you get?
FORTNITER #2: It's Dynamite.
FORTNITER #1: Yeah, but which one?
FORTNITER #2: Never mind.

•

How does a *Fortnite* player turn on a TV?
With an emote control.

WHAT KIND OF DINOSAUR
PLAYS FORTNITE?

A FLOSSIRAPTOR.

How many Fortniters does it take to change a lightbulb?
Two. One to change the bulb and the other to dance for a
minute.

•

FORTNITER #1: Watch out for the moat!
FORTNITER #2: Where?
**FORTNITER #1: At the end of the game. An *e*mote. I'm
a terrible dancer.**

CHAPTER 6
KNOCK-KNOCKED

Don't get knocked by these Fortnite *knock-knock jokes.*

Knock-knock!
Who's there?
Brutus.
Brutus who?
**Brutus some coffee so we can stay up late and play
    Fortnite!**

●

Knock-knock!
Who's there?
Bullseye.
Bullseye who?
Bullseye think I know where we dropping!

Knock-knock!
Who's there?
Cole.
Cole who?
Cole out here, let me in before I freeze!

●

KNOCK-KNOCK!
WHO'S THERE?
ANITA.
ANITA WHO?
ANITA BORROW SOME V-BUCKS!

Knock-knock!
Who's there?
Hybrid.
Hybrid who?
Hybrid you open the door please?

●

Knock-knock!
Who's there?
Paradox.
Paradox who?
Paradox here to examine your battle wounds.

●

Knock-knock!
Who's there?
Lexa.
Lexa who?
Lexa go play Fortnite.

Knock-knock!
Who's there?
Zoey.
Zoey who?
Zoey gonna play *Fortnite* or what?

Knock-knock!
Who's there?
Verge.
Verge who?
Verge who's like commitment to your squad will serve you well in *Fortnite*!

•

Knock-knock!
Who's there?
Triple Threat.
Triple Threat who?
Knock-knock!
Who's there?
Triple Threat.
Triple Threat who?

Knock-knock!
Who's there?
Triple Threat.
Triple Threat who?
I've made my point.

Knock-knock!
Who's there?
Rush.
Rush who?
Hey, not so fast.

Knock-knock!
Who's there?
Peakaboo.
Peekaboo who?
Hey, don't cry!

Knock-knock!
Who's there?
Maven.
Maven who?
Maven you want to play *Fortnite* with me?

•

Knock-knock!
Who's there?
Hime.
Hime who?
Hime who you think it is!

•

KNOCK-KNOCK!
WHO'S THERE?
X MARK.
X MARK WHO?
X MARK THE SPOT!

Knock-knock!
Who's there?
Heidi.
Heidi who?
Heidi who, neighborino!

●

Knock-knock!
Who's there?
Hay Man.
Hay Man who?
Hay Man, good game!

●

Knock-knock!
Who's there?
Havoc.
Havoc who?
Havoc your way!

Knock-knock!
Who's there?
Far Out Man.
Far Out Man who?
Far Out Man who came all this way.

•

Knock-knock!
Who's there?
Island.
Island who?
Island-ed in Homely Hills!

•

Knock-knock!
Who's there?
Thor.
Thor who?
Thtill Thor I beat you in *Fortnite*?

Knock-knock!
Who's there?
Menace.
Menace who?
Menace to the other *Fortnite* players!

●

Knock-knock!
Who's there?
Mave.
Mave who?
Mave you'll get lucky in the Battle Royale.

●

Knock-knock!
Who's there?
Turk.
Turk who?
Turk who dinner for Thanksgiving!

Knock-knock!
Who's there?
V-Bucks.
V bucks who?
V-Bucks full of loot are yours for the taking!

●

Knock-knock!
Who's there?
Ice King.
Ice King who?
Ice King if you want to play *Fortnite*?

●

Knock-knock!
Who's there?
Ark.
Ark who?
"Ark the herald angels sing!"

Knock-knock!
Who's there?
Deadeye.
Deadeye who?
Deadeye do that?

Knock-knock!
Who's there?
Deadfire.
Deadfire who?
Deadfire on you, did I?

Knock-knock!
Who's there?
Flytrap.
Flytrap who?
Flytrap you and then knock you.

KNOCK-KNOCK!
WHO'S THERE?
ARROW.
ARROW WHO?
ARROW ON THE SIDE OF CAUTION.

Knock-knock!

Who's there?

Omen.

Omen who?

Omen, I can't believe I got knocked out so fast!

Knock-knock!
Who's there?
Blitz.
Blitz who?
Blitz get on the Battle Bus right now!

●

Knock-knock!
Who's there?
Hay Man.
Hay Man who?
Hay Man, why'd you eliminate me?

●

Knock-knock!
Who's there?
Heidi.
Heidi who?
I didn't know you could yodel!

Knock-knock!
Who's there?
Nite Nite.
Nite Nite who?
Hey, stop clowning around.

•

Knock-knock!
Who's there?
Vix.
Vix who?
Vix your mats and let's go!

•

Knock-knock!
Who's there?
Cube Brute.
Cube Brute who?
The Cube Brute of 8 is 2!

Knock-knock!
Who's there?
Ice Fiend.
Ice Fiend who?
I scream, you scream, we all scream for Ice Fiend!

•

Knock-knock!
Who's there?
Ellie.
Ellie who?
Elevator, look out for IO Guards!

•

Knock-knock!
Who's there?
Ice Throne.
Ice Throne who?
Ice Throne, where'd you get it?

Knock-knock!
Who's there?
Shiver Inn.
Shiver Inn who?
Shiver Inn out here, can you let me in?

●

Knock-knock!
Who's there?
Arrow.
Arrow who?
Arrow't of the game, let's start over.

●

Knock-knock!
Who's there?
An arrow.
An arrow who?
An arrow victory is still a victory!

Knock-knock!
Who's there?
Kit.
Kit who?
Just kitting!

•

Knock-knock!
Who's there?
Weeping Woods.
Weeping Woods who?
Weeping wood make you feel better if you're feeling fad.

•

Knock-knock!
Who's there?
Norway.
Norway who?
Norway I'm staying out here with these Husks!

Knock-knock!
Who's there?
Holly Hedges.
Holly Hedges who?
**Holly hedges by trying to land in as safe a spot as
   possible.**

•

Knock-knock!
Who's there?
Cube.
Cube who?
Hey, don't cry, Kevin!

•

Knock-Knock
Who's there?
Flint-Knock.
Flint-Knock who?
Hey, I thought *I* was the one knocking.

Knock-knock!
Who's there?
Chest.
Chest who?
Chest kidding!

●

Knock-knock!
Who's there?
Loot.
Loot who?
Loot do you want me to be?

●

Knock-knock!
Who's there?
Minnie.
Minnie who?
Mini-Shield!

Knock-knock!

Who's there?

Carry.

Carry who?

Carrying my squad to victory!

•

KNOCK-KNOCK!
WHO'S THERE?
TEEF.
TEEF WHO?
TEEF HURT AFTER THE DENTIST!

Knock-knock!
Who's there?
Duo.
Duo who?
Duover!

●

Knock-knock!
Who's there?
Raptor.
Raptor who?
Raptor, just listening to your victory story.

●

Knock-knock!
Who's there?
Shield.
Shield who?
Shield do for our squad!

Knock-knock!
Who's there?
Cube.
Cube who?
Cube be taking forever to get to the lobby!

●

Knock-knock!
Who's there?
Knock-knock.
Knock-knock who?
You're knock-knocked out!

●

Knock-knock!
Who's there?
Ave Axe.
Ave Axe who?
**Ave Axe you once again, do you want to play *Fortnite* or
    not?**

●

Knock-knock!
Who's there?
Axe.
Axe who?
Axe-ercise would be good for us.

●

Knock-knock!
Who's there?
Chocollama.
Chocollama who?
Chocollama ding dong!

●

Knock-knock!
Who's there?
Chew.
Chew who?
Chew who, here I am!

Knock-knock!
Who's there?
Knockwurst.
Knockwurst who?
Knocked-worst is knocked early.

•

Knock-knock!
Who's there?
Lamp.
Lamp who?
Lamp who all over this field, gross!

•

Knock-knock!
Who's there?
Lawnbreaker.
Lawnbreaker who?
Lawnbreakers belong in the Prison!

Knock-knock!
Who's there?
Axe.
Axe who?
Axe anybody!

•

Knock-knock!
Who's there?
Purr Axe.
Purr Axe who?
Purr Axe we'll drop right here?

•

Knock-knock!
Who's there?
Talon.
Talon who?
I'm Talon you, I'm great at *Fortnite*.

Knock-knock!
Who's there?
Night Hawk.
Night Hawk who?
Good night to you, too.

●

Knock-knock!
Who's there?
Behold.
Behold who?
Behold my dancing!

●

Knock-knock!
Who's there?
Burpee.
Burpee who?
Excuse me.

Knock-knock!
Who's there?
Hello Friend!
Hello Friend who?
It's me!
Oh, hi!

●

Knock-knock!
Who's there?
IDK.
IDK who?
IDK either!

●

Knock-knock!
Who's there?
Mark.
Mark who?
On your Mark . . .

Knock-knock!
Who's there?
Hime.
Hime who?
Hime gonna beat you at *Fortnite*.

•

Knock-knock!
Who's there?
Poki.
Poki who?
***Pokémon* is out, *Fortnite* is in.**

•

Knock-knock!
Who's there?
Poof.
Poof who?
I poof-who *Fortnite Creative*, not *Battle Royale*.

Knock-knock!
Who's there?
Skipper.
Skipper who?
Skipper your chores to play *Fortnite* again?

•

Knock-knock!
Who's there?
Snap.
Snap who?
Snap-who at Epic left everybody with free V-Bucks!

•

Knock-knock!
Who's there?
Snow Day.
Snow Day who?
Snow Day like today to play *Fortnite*!

Knock-knock!
Who's there?
Take the Cake.
Take the Cake who?
Take the Cake to my house!

●

Knock-knock!
Who's there?
Tidy.
Tidy who?
Tidy who to you!

●

Knock-knock!
Who's there?
Time Out.
Time Out who?
Time Out! My mom needs me.

KNOCK-KNOCK!
WHO'S THERE?
INTERRUPTING MOUNTAIN
INTERRUPTING MOUN—
VOLCANO!

Knock-knock!
Who's there?
Waterworks.
Waterworks who?
Hey, don't cry!

●

Knock-knock!
Who's there?
Welcome.
Welcome who?
Welcome you!

●

Knock-knock!
Who's there?
Olive.
Olive who?
Olived on The Island until they got turned into Husks.

Knock-knock!
Who's there?
Athena.
Athena who?
Athena chest near here before.

●

Knock-knock!
Who's there?
Eileen.
Eileen who?
Eileen on my weapon and it fired.

●

Knock-knock!
Who's there?
Rhoda.
Rhoda who?
Rhoda Battle Bus to get here.

Knock-knock!
Who's there?
Frida.
Frida who?
Frida Husks, open up!

●

Knock-knock!
Who's there?
Lois.
Lois who?
Lois on the standings this time, #100 if you can believe it!

●

Knock-knock!
Who's there?
Hannah.
Hannah who?
Hannah we get that launcher?

Knock-knock!
Who's there?
Tamara.
Tamara who?
Tamara we'll play *Fortnite* again.

•

Knock-knock!
Who's there?
May.
May who?
May-lee starting!

•

Knock-knock!
Who's there?
Gwen.
Gwen who?
Gwen do you think the new *Fortnite* season will start?

Knock-knock!
Who's there?
Wooden.
Wooden who?
Wooden you like to know!

•

Knock-knock!
Who's there?
Mini.
Mini who?
Mini open your mouth, you get silly!

•

Knock-knock!
Who's there?
Husk.
Husk who?
Bless you!

Knock-knock!
Who's there?
Brick.
Brick who?
Brick or treat!

Knock-knock!
Who's there?
Battle.
Battle who?
Battle not let me die out here, squad!

Knock-knock!
Who's there?
Apple.
Apple who?
Apple on the door but it won't budge!

Knock-knock!
Who's there?
Beef.
Beef who?
Beef-ore I win again, you should just quit!

•

Knock-knock!
Who's there?
Norma Lee.
Norma Lee who?
Norma Lee my emote is The Robot.

•

Knock-Knock!
Who's there?
Criss.
Criss who?
Criss Cross!

Knock-knock!
Who's there?
Pear.
Pear who?
Pear-a-chuting in!

•

Knock-knock!
Who's there?
Blue.
Blue who?
Blue is my favorite potion color.

•

Knock-knock!
Who's there?
Cart.
Cart who.
I can feel my cart pounding!

Knock-knock!
Who's there?
Llama piñata.
Beat it!

●

KNOCK-KNOCK!
WHO'S THERE?
MUSHROOM.
MUSHROOM WHO?
THERE'S MUSHROOM FOR IMPROVEMENT
WITH THAT LAST JOKE.

Knock-knock!
Who's there?
Decay.
Decay who?
Decay is de problem with de Husks.

•

Knock-knock!
Who's there?
Ammo.
Ammo who?
Ammo gonna beat you today!

•

Knock-knock!
Who's there?
Default.
Default who?
Not my default you don't have any skins.

Knock-knock!
Who's there?
Thermal.
Thermal who?
Thermal replaced Retail Row.

CHAPTER 7
WORDPLAY

Silly fun abounds — even for Fortnite *noobs!*

Fortnite Tongue Twisters

"Slowly shrinking circles!" she shrugged.

A Husk musk must hurt.

The Nurse is for sure worse than a ho-hum Husk.

I ran right around a rare ripe Ripper!

"Sky Stalker stalked seven skies," so Supersonic says.

Polar Patroller popped Peekabo's plans, poof!

Rapscallion wraps scallions around battalions of stallions.

THE TRUTH ABOUT SLEUTH
IS THAT HE'S PROFUSELY ALOOF.

Great Grottos grow green, gamer!

I couldn't figure out which way Witch Way went, so I
switched with Mitch for a Flamenco and a Flamingo.

SHE SAW SNACKS
AT THE STACK SHACK.

●

Fortnite Anagrams

We rearranged the letters in the names of some *Fortnite* locations, characters, and emotes. Can you arrange the letters back to find the answers? The answers can be found on pages 148-149.

1. Twitter lodes
    Wilted otters

2. Trailer ow!
   Lair tower

3. Hey, dog shell
   Yodel gel? Shh!

4. Tricky odds
   Dry kid cots

5. Meaty wisdoms
   Mess to midway

6. Rumply wasps
   Spy lumps war

7. Wowed pigeons
   Wide sewn goop

8. Uh, lofty scarf!
   Fact: Hours fly.

9. Stay, Ed's swan!
   Sad yawn sets

10. BOB'S FEES
    BEES' FOBS

11. Messy attacks
    Cats' sky meats

12. Glassy prints
    Pastry slings

13. A made tooth
    Mad hate, too

14. I add reef
    Fair deed

15. Of punks
    Fop sunk

16. BURN, NARY BLEW
    NEW YARN BLURB

17. MRS. CHOP
    MS. PORCH

18. Shag burner
    She brag runs

19. Flown user
    Elf runs, ow!

20. Lilac aprons
    I ran, scallop!

21. Her cow prod
    Or porch dew!

22. Junky, nor bees
    Bye, noun jerks!

23. Sock chart
    Arch stock

24. Meter flares
    Fear smelter

25. Freight rigs
    Her first gig

26. Dopey hinter
    Elder python

27. Tinier pin spot
    Inspire tip ton

28. Otter fin
    Ten for it

Answers:
1. Tilted Towers
2. Retail Row
3. Holly Hedges
4. Dirty Docks
5. Misty Meadows
6. Slurpy Swamp
7. Weeping Woods
8. Flush Factory
9. Sweaty Sands
10. Beef Boss
11 Steamy Stacks
12. Salty Springs
13. Tomatohead
14. Deadfire
15. Bunny Brawler
16. Funk Ops
17. Chomp Sr.
18. Bushranger
19. Sunflower
20. Rapscallion
21. Power Chord
22. Bunker Jonesy

23. Crackshot
24. Farmer Steel
25. Triggerfish
26. Ride the Pony
27. Pristine Point
28. *Fortnite*

•

Fortnite Opposites

Can you name the Fortnite location based on the words that mean the opposite of their names? The answers can be found on page 150.

1. The Completes
2. Big Animal Hovel
3. Doggy Round
4. Harmless Skies
5. Steamy Shipments
6. Straight City
7. Peppery Shacks
8. Dry Waters
9. Slender Middle
10. Remarkable Towers

AN UNOFFICIAL JOKE BOOK FOR FORTNITERS

11. Upright Meadows
12. Wide-Open Weakspot

Answers:
1. The Ruins
2. Ant Manor
3. Catty Corner
4. Fatal Fields
5. Frosty Flights
6. Tilted Town
7. Salty Towers
8. Sweaty Sands
9. Stumpy Ridge
10. Unremarkable Shack
11. Weeping Woods
12. Stealthy Stronghold

●

They Said What?

"Do you have any Harvesting Tools?" Omega axed.

"I need to fix that Chopping Chart," said Raven mechanically.

"I need a new axe," Brite Bomber said bluntly.

"I got one-pumped three times," said the *Fortnite* player triumphantly.

"I forgot to put a door on my structure," said Red Knight openly.

"This Durr Burger burger is hard to chew," Desperado beefed jerkily.

"I just threw a grenade!" boomed Calamity.

"I have two dozen V-Bucks minus two," said the *Fortnite* player tensely.

151

"I shall use my hammer," said Thor bashfully.

"I'm a banana man!" said Peely appealingly.

"Give me that arrow," said Burnout with a bow.

"I've never crashed my Quad Crasher," said Renegade Raider recklessly.

"I want to get those monsters!" said Sleuth in a husky voice.

"I'm excellent at finding wood," said the *Fortnite* player lumberingly.

"I used to control other flying things," the Battle Bus driver explained.

"This balloon is full of hot air," the Battle Bus driver belched.

"Who chopped down this tree?" asked Musha, stumped.

"I like the skin that looks like a crow," said the *Fortnite* player ravenously.

"Stay out of my gold bars!" Warpaint claimed.

"This boat sank, but at least my hat fits," said Birdie, capsized.

"Those Hive Husks stung me!" said Highland Warrior begrudgingly.

"What a B.R.U.T.E.," said Bear Force One mechanically.

"That's the last time I try to touch a Husk," said Ginger Gunner offhandedly.

"I'll be taking that loot," said Enforcer appropriately.

"I'm at high ground!" Magnus alleged.

"Here's your V-Bucks for the next week," the parent advanced.

"I like Bunny Brawler," said the *Fortnite* player acutely.

"Nobody here anymore," the Hive Husk said belatedly.

"I built a winding staircase," said Clinical Crosser coyly.

"I need to sharpen my sword," said Shade bluntly.

"Time to get supplies for Durr Burger milkshakes," Cuddle Team Leader uttered.

"There are 100 people in this lobby," the *Fortnite* player recounted.

"The Storm is coming," said Oblivion darkly.

"I set up the electric fence," said Whiteout amply.

"I can't believe I finished in third place," said the *Fortnite* player anticlimactically.

"Look at those Husklings," said Chomp Sr. shortly.

"Oops! There goes my hat!" said Pastel off the top of her head.

"I'm going to grow my hair out," said Backbone baldly.

"Who wants consumables?" Dazzle asked cornily.

"I'm an extremely accurate marksman," said Rex arrow-gantly.

"THE STORM HASN'T HIT YET," BREATHED VALKYRIE AIRILY.

"Please don't point that arrow at me," said Sgt. Green Clover, quivering.

"The Battle Bus Tires are too big," said Circuit Breaker under pressure.

"Hey, who shattered my window?" asked Dominator painfully.

"I have the whole Island map memorized," said the pathologist.

"Hooray for our squad!" said the *Fortnite* player cheerfully.

●

You know you play too much *Fortnite* when . . .

. . . you're running and you suddenly start bunny hopping.

. . . you eat your cereal out of a big pot.

. . . you need to tie your shoes and you say, "Aim down sight!"

. . . someone does something well you tell them, "Hey, goated on the sticks!"

. . . you drink Orange Justice for breakfast.

. . . you're going upstairs and you say you're "heading for high ground."

. . . you're going downstairs and you say you're "getting Harry Pottered."

. . . you walk into a crowded room, you say, "Hot drop!"

. . . you call every basketball court "LeBron's house."

. . . you fill your school backpack with "mats."

. . . you call your chewable vitamins "meds."

. . . you write a text and say "FULL SEND."

. . . you're alone with another person and you call it "1 v. 1."

. . . you put away your clothes and you say you've "vaulted" them.

. . . you play by yourself in band, you stand up and yell, "Solo Kill!"

. . . someone says "season's greetings" and you think they mean a new season of Fortnite is out.

. . . you ask your smart speaker, "Lexa, give me *Fortnite* tips."

. . . you go out for breakfast and order Mancakes.

. . . you don't run errands, you take "side quests."

. . . you get on a plane and ask to see the hot air balloon.

. . . you want all your food to be "Salty."

. . . you see there's a storm in the forecast and you prepare yourself.

. . . every time you open the fridge door, you brace for a Riot Husky.

. . . you will not go anywhere *near* a corn husk.

. . . you husk corn by completely destroying it from across the room.

. . . you top a wrapped present with a crossbow.

. . . you think about joining the Galaxy Scouts.

. . . it's summer vacation, and you're more interested in a loot pool than a swimming pool.

. . . you don't call it a bathroom, it's a "Flush Factory."

. . . you always want to be skins in "shirts vs. skins" games.

. . . you get on the school bus and ask, "Where we dropping today?"

. . . you get a gold star in class and get disappointed because you thought they said "gold scar."

. . . you don't put on deodorant, you use a potion.

. . . you don't use a swab to clean your ears, you're "utilizing a Harvesting Tool."

. . . you look at your utensils and see "fork, knife."

. . . you call your Halloween costume a "limited edition skin."

. . . you've tried to pay for something in the real world with V-Bucks.

. . . you call blue sports drink Slurp Juice.

. . . you call your dad "Ice Pop."

. . . you tried to join the Storm Scouts.

. . . you don't drink water, you "Big Chuggus" it.

. . . you call a can of Pringles "Chipwreck Towers."

. . . you see your dad shaving, and you think he's "headed to Razor Crest."

. . . your favorite class is Advanced Math.

. . . husky dogs freak you out.

. . . you signed up to be a Drum Major without really knowing what it would involve.

. . . your parents ask you to water the grass and you use the Sprinkler.

. . . you feel bad about having a friend named Matt, because you just want to see if he can give you stuff.

. . . you don't buy new clothes, you get new skins.

. . . you think you might name your daughter G. G.

. . . you didn't "wake up like this," it's your "default player."

. . . you refer to any couple as a duo or a squad.

SCAR LIGHT, SCAR BRIGHT
FIRST SCAR I SEE TONIGHT
I WISH I COULD, AND I JUST MIGHT
BEAT ALL MY TEAMMATES TO IT, THAT
WOULD BE ALRIGHT!

CHAPTER 8
WHERE WE DROPPING?

Where we dropping Fortnite *jokes too goofy and weird for any other chapter? Right here.*

What should you wear if you're really trying hard to win at *Fortnite*?
A sweater.

•

In real life, you sit on a tack and it hurts.
In *Fortnite*, you find a Tac and it's great!

•

Where do Fortniters sleep best?
On yeets!

•

How do cows start a game of *Battle Royale*?
They board the Cattle Bus.

How do babies play *Fortnite*?
They get on the Rattle Bus.

•

Did you hear that the Queen started playing *Fortnite*?
She likes *Battle Royal*.

•

Why do dentists like *Fortnite*?
Because everybody flosses all the time.

•

Do only kids play *Fortnite*?
No, adults love it too, especially if they're in their 90s.

•

Why can't you use "Fortnite" as your *Fortnite* password?
It's two week.

•

Did you hear the new season of *Fortnite* was delayed for technical issues?
Talk about an Epic fail!

DID YOU HEAR ABOUT THE
BARNYARD ANIMAL WHO LEARNED
TO PLAY FORTNITE?

SHE WON THE CATTLE ROYALE!

They should build security fences out of *Fortnite*.
Nobody can seem to get over it!

•

Did you hear about the sequel to *Fortnite*?
It's called *Month*.

•

Why were there 41 characters in season 2 of *Fortnite*?
Because 42 would be too many!

•

What's the name of the Battle Bus driver?
Battle Gus!

•

How come people who work in stores are good at *Fortnite*?
They know how to tag.

•

I thought I'd just temporarily like *Fortnite*.
Like I'd only be interested in it for two weeks.

Have you ever done rubber banding in *Fortnite*?
Oh, it's a snap.

●

WHERE IN SWEATY SANDS WOULD
YOU STILL FIND PIRATES?

THE ARRGH-V PARK.

What's a Fortniter's favorite season?
New *Fortnite* season.

●

What's a Fortniter's *other* favorite season?
Salty Spring.

●

How is *Fortnite* like the X-Men?
Storm is on the way.

●

**Did you hear about the Fortniters who robbed the
    alphabet factory?**
They took the L.

●

How is *Fortnite* different from a really hard math class?
One has a Battle Pass and one takes a battle to pass.

●

Why are ball-hogs no good at *Fortnite*?
They never Battle Pass.

Where did the time-traveling Fortniter go first?
The 90s!

●

I play *Fortnite* so much my friends miss me.
But their aim is getting better.

●

FORTNITER #1: Are you ever going to get around to playing one of those special *Fortnite* quests?
FORTNITER #2: Oh, event-ually.

●

How is *Fortnite* unlike any other computer game?
It *begins* with a crash.

●

Why did the royal *Fortnite* player sleep in a castle at night?
Because that was his fort right!

FORTNITER #1: My pencil went all *Fortnite*.
FORTNITER #2: What do you mean?
FORTNITER #1: It has Zero Point.

●

Why was the Fortniter running away instead of camping?
Because fort-une favors the brave!

●

Why was the *Fortniter* not putting in any effort?
Because all they were after was The Big Chill.

●

What did the chef name her *Fortnite* restaurant?
Butter Royale.

●

Where do Fortniters sleep?
In a nite fort!

Did you hear about the dumb Fortniter?
He didn't want to play because he'd never played *Onenite,*
Twonite, and *Threenite.*

●

I lost eight pounds playing *Fortnite*
I'm English, so that's about $10.

●

What do *Fortnite* and ghosts have in common?
No blood and guts.

●

***Fortnite* may be a new game . . .**
. . . But it's stuck in the 90s.

●

What *Fortnite* creature would be great in math class?
Butterflies, because they're always multiplying!

What happens to a scout that gets caught in the rain?
They become a Storm Scout.

•

Why don't Fortniters like autumn?
They hate the fall!

•

What do Fortniters call leaves on the ground?
Fall damage.

•

No matter how good you are at *Fortnite* . . .
. . . you're still bush league.

•

Admit it: You're reading this right now because you died first in *Battle Royale* and you're waiting for your squad to finish up.

•

What's sweatier than Sweaty Sands?
When you're down to 1 vs. 1.

What do golf and *Fortnite* have in common?

They're both full of traps and woods.

HOW CAN YOU LOSE A GAME OF
FORTNITE BEFORE IT EVEN BEGAN?

IF YOU GET BATTLE BUS-TED.

What do floppers wear on their feet?
Flop-flops.

●

FORTNITER #1: Why are you feeling blue?
FORTNITER #2: Storm's coming.

●

How is _Fortnite_ like being a toddler?
Winding up in the corner is a terrible punishment.

●

When is a jar scary?
When a door is ajar in your house in _Fortnite_.

●

You ever eliminated somebody in _Fortnite_?
Hey, don't knock it till you tried it.

●

Fortnite isn't like real life.
Fire heals you.
But rain kills you?

When is the best month to play *Fortnite*?
May-lee.

•

I have a good attitude about winning.
Come what melee!

•

I'll take the L . . .
. . . But I'm not sure where I'm supposed to take it.

•

What are *Fortnite* #SquadGoals?
Being the only person left in your squad.

•

How do you get your friend Ron to be in your squadron?
Say, "Want to join the squad, Ron?"

•

What do a *Fortnite* noob and a door have in common?
They're easily knocked.

WHAT TYPE OF FORTNITE DO
HORSES PLAY?

SADDLE ROYALE.

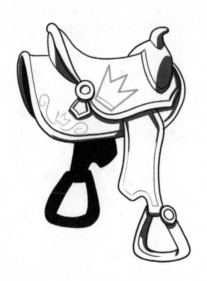

●

Are there bankers in *Fortnite*?

Sure, anybody who gets knocked will leave you "a loan."

What did the Fortniter with a cough take?
Drops.

•

I got to high ground and still got knocked.
I guess I just had a bad altitude.

•

When you think about it,
Fortnite is really a game of shirts and skins.

•

Do teachers like *Fortnite*?
Sure, it builds character!

•

When does two weeks take about 20 minutes?
When it's a game of *Fortnite*.

•

FORTNITER #1: Did you like the Volcano Event?
FORTNITER #2: I didn't lava it.

The End is the end, but what comes at the end of The End?

The letter "d."

·

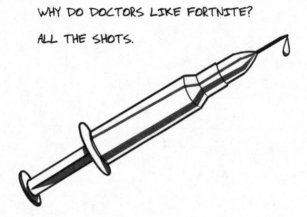

WHY DO DOCTORS LIKE FORTNITE?

ALL THE SHOTS.

·

When is the end not the end?

In *Fortnite*.

Did you hear the joke about The End?
Never mind, we're past that.

•

What type of *Fortnite* do dairy cows play?
Butter Royale.

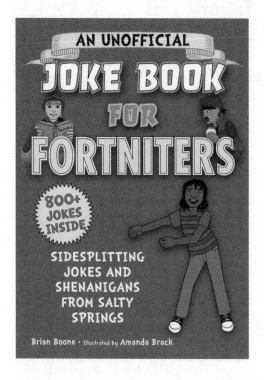